LE
Corbusier

To Thomas and Harry

THIS IS A CARLTON BOOK

Text and design copyright © 2000 Carlton Books Limited

This edition published by Carlton Books Limited 2000
20 Mortimer Street
London
W1N 7RD

www.carltonbooks.com

A CIP catalogue for this book is available from the Library of Congress

ISBN 1 85868 963 5

Printed and bound in Dubai

LE
Corbusier

ELIZABETH DARLING

CARLTON
BOOKS

Le Corbusier

is the most revered – and reviled – of twentieth-century architects. For many he is the greatest of architects, the beauty and scope of his work – from architecture to furniture design, town planning to painting – assuring him of this position. For others his all-encompassing vision of design is perceived as a stylistic megalomania and he is much maligned for the influence his work had on the reconstruction of our cities and housing in the decades after 1945.

Whether hero or villain, Corbusier was unquestionably the most significant and influential of twentieth-century architects. As such his work should never be dismissed. It may be challenging, but it is always worthy of closer analysis. Perhaps then we can go some way to understanding why, over a century after his birth, this extraordinary man continues to invoke both admiration and anger.

"A GREAT EPOCH HAS BEGUN. THERE EXISTS A NEW spirit"

Born towards the end of the nineteenth century Corbusier came to adulthood in the twentieth, and it was his perception of what this new century represented that would guide the development of his architecture. For Corbusier the twentieth century was a machine age, dominated by engineering technology and mass production. This was an era of internationalism, mass communication, mass democracy and science. Its defining forms were the car, the aeroplane and ocean liner.

In this new century Corbusier saw progress in all aspects of life; all aspects, that is, except architecture. Instead of advancing with and responding to these exciting changes, architecture was stuck in the nineteenth century and was concerned only with debates over which historical style it was most appropriate to revive. Its progress had been arrested and it was, Corbusier declared, "in an unhappy state of retrogression".

It thus became Corbusier's mission to wrest architecture from its stylistic impasse and

LE COR

replace it with a movement whose forms were as modern and revolutionary as the new century. Corbusier was not alone in his desire to create a new architecture. His ideas formed part of the Modern Movement and his work was contemporary with that of the other great modernists, Walter Gropius and Mies van der Rohe. Only Corbusier, however, made such a definitive mark on the twentieth century.

Like Gropius and Mies, Corbusier looked to the products and methods of the engineer for inspiration for the forms the new architecture might take. In what he called the "Engineer's Aesthetic" he saw a simplicity and standardization of forms, as well as a logical method of design that addressed issues of function not style, which he believed

"ARCHITECTURE IS STIFLED BY CUSTOM. THE styles ARE A LIE."

could form the basis of a new approach to architecture. But he was also insistent on the need to combine the Engineer's Aesthetic with the underlying essentials of architecture. These had nothing to do with style, but were the permanent and timeless values that underpinned all good architecture: volume, surface and plan.

For Corbusier, it was only through a marriage of the definitively modern with ancient and traditional values that a permanent revolution in design could take place and a modern architecture arise.

Corbusier's emergence as a modern architect can be dated to the early 1920s with the publication of his "manifesto", *Vers une Architecture* (translated in English as *Towards a New Architecture*) in 1923. To reach the stage where he was able both to conceptualize the need for, and the form of, a new architecture was, as the manifesto's title suggests, a gradual process. He did not set out to create a modern architecture, but looking back from 1923 he was able to see his earlier developments in these terms. And once he had defined his goal, it remained with him throughout his life.

BUSIER

TOWARDS A NEW ARCHITECTURE

Corbusier was born in the Swiss town of La Chaux-de-Fonds in 1887, his given name Charles-Edouard Jeanneret (for simplicity's sake I shall refer to him as Corbusier throughout this text). His family background was artistic, but not wealthy, and, like many in Chaux, he was expected to work in some way for the local industry, watch-making. So, in 1902, he was sent to the town's school of arts and crafts where he trained to become an engraver and designer of watch cases.

Even at this early date, Corbusier was absorbing ideas which would inform his later work. Under its director, Charles L'Eplattenier, the art school in Chaux taught with Arts and Crafts principles, one of the first movements in nineteenth-century design to shed the conventions of the past. L'Eplattenier encouraged his students to create a vocabulary of decoration by looking to natural forms in which the mountainside town of Chaux was rich. They were taught to reduce these to their underlying forms rather than to represent them naturalistically. The resulting abstract shapes would then constitute a basic grammar of form and ornament for the applied arts and architecture.

This approach can be seen in Corbusier's first work as an architect, the Villa Fallet of 1906. Designed in collaboration with a local architect, Rene Chapallaz, it is a pure piece of arts and crafts architecture in its adaptation and simplification of vernacular traditions. Its form alludes to the chalet – the traditional style of architecture in the area – while the decorative design on the facades was a schematized representation of the forest site in which the house stood.

In Chaux, Corbusier absorbed the first of the principles that would govern his life's work. L'Eplattenier imbued in him a search for essentials, for underlying constants of form, and the equation of the modern with the simplification of forms. His background also left him with an abiding love of nature.

The commission for the Villa Fallet was a turning point for Corbusier. Henceforth, he would commit himself to architecture. Over the next ten years he embarked on a journey of self education that exposed him to the twin influences of tradition and modernity.

On what he called his "*Voyage d' Orient*", he encountered the buildings of antiquity for the first time; a profound experience. In Rome he was struck by the bold use of structure, shape and volume in the Pantheon, and in Athens by the Parthenon. This seemed to him to be the perfect "type": a work of the highest order, concerned with essential values, its perfection recalling the precision and exactitude of the engineer. His studies of these classical buildings also taught him about the centrality of systems of proportion and harmony to their design.

He also saw, on a visit to the Carthusian monastery at Ema in Tuscany, a simplified form of dwelling that he would later use to considerable effect. At Ema, each monk lived in an enclosed double height cell, each with its own garden. He was especially struck by the integration of nature into a sheltered living space.

Between 1908 and 1910 Corbusier received his first formal architectural training in the offices of the leading modern architects of the day: Auguste Perret and Peter Behrens. From Perret he absorbed the doctrine of reinforced concrete as the material of the twentieth century and a reverence for the French classical tradition. Behrens, on the other hand, taught Corbusier to equate the modern with the machine. He also introduced Corbusier to the ideas of the German design reform group, the Deutsche Werkbund, of which he was a leading member. This meant that Corbusier became conversant with its preoccupation with mass production and the development of "standard types" to facilitate this process. A later encounter with the other great early modern architect, Tony Garnier, would also prove significant. When Corbusier met him, he was working on his unrealized plan for a new layout and form for an urbanized and industrialized city, La Cité Industrielle. This attempt to create a modern form for the city, to be built entirely from reinforced concrete, perhaps suggested such a concept to Corbusier for the first time.

Corbusier's first attempts to translate these influences into a more modern form of architecture came in 1915 and 1916. No doubt drawing from the idea of standardization he had learnt in Berlin he developed a basic house type – the Maison Dom-Ino – made from reinforced concrete and intended for mass-production. By calling it Dom-Ino Corbusier was indicating that the house was as standardized but also as flexible in use as a domino counter. It consisted of a reinforced concrete frame with concrete floor slabs that were cantilevered over the columns of the frame. This was a basic constructional unit that could be repeated endlessly, and whose interior could be arranged as the occupant wished since none of the walls had to be loadbearing.

In 1916, Corbusier designed the Villa Schwob in La Chaux-de-Fonds that demonstrated a dramatic break with his previous arts and crafts-inspired work. For the first time he employed a reinforced concrete frame, similar to his recently developed Dom-Ino system. Equally significantly, the house owed more to the classical architecture he had seen on his travels than the vernacular. Corbusier based the plan on the primary geometrical forms of the circle and the square arranged symmetrically on an alternating system of wide and narrow bays. The facade is simple, with a minimal use of classical detailing. Inside, the main living area of the house is a double height space; an early use of the type of interior Corbusier had seen at the monastery in Ema.

Though this Villa had a modern structure, Corbusier's visual language was still an historical one, albeit simplified. To be able to create the architectural language to match the modernity of his constructional techniques required Corbusier to embark on another journey. In 1916, he returned to Paris.

It was the experiments in art which had taken place in Paris that provided Corbusier with the catalyst to break from the styles of the past. Cubism's break with representation and its fragmentation of space inspired him. It is not surprising then that it was with an artist, Amédée Ozenfant, that Corbusier worked to create a new architectural language, which they called Purism. Its main thesis was the need for the conscious refinement of all existing types; the rejection of detail both in shape and ornament. Although the two men initially applied this theory to painting, it was intended as an all embracing aesthetic system, applicable to all the arts: from product design to architecture.

Ozenfant and Corbusier promoted the new doctrine of Purism through the pages of *L' Esprit Nouveau*, a magazine which they began to edit in 1920. It was to coincide with this commitment to a new aesthetic that the former Charles-Edouard Jeanneret adopted the pseudonym Le Corbusier. Finally, he had reached the point at which a new architecture could emerge; its arrival heralded by the publication of *Vers une Architecture*.

A PURIST ARCHITECTURE

In *Vers une Architecture* Corbusier wrote, "Modern life demands, and is waiting for, a new kind of plan, both for the house and the city". Through Purism architecture could catch up with modern life.

For Corbusier, as already noted, modern life was analogous to the machine. As compartmentalized, standardized and efficient as the ass embly line which manufactured the mass-produced objects, Purism would, in Corbusier's mind, meet the demands of modern life. It provided the means to reform architecture both visually and spatially and would form the theoretical spine of all Corbusier's subsequent architecture. It reflects his marriage of the principles of engineering and architectural principles, the concepts of modernity and tradition, to which he had been exposed on his journey of self education.

Inspired by the products of the machine he pursued an interest in designing "types": both for the house and the city. From modern art, he took abstraction as the basis of his architectural language; from architectural tradition, the idea of underlying constants of form and systems of rules to govern the design and appearance of his architecture: from the "Five Points of a New Architecture" of 1926, the modern equivalent of the five orders of classical architecture, to "the Modulor" of 1950, a new system of proportion.

With this approach, Corbusier sought to replace the chaos of contemporary architecture. His ultimate aim was to allow man, machine and nature to co-exist in a state of equilibrium. The result was what might best be termed a "machine-age classicism".

In his first decade of practice Corbusier's attention focused primarily on the house and its contents. Much of this work began as theory, and was expounded in the pages of *Vers une Architecture*. There can be found a number of the house-types which Corbusier envisaged could revolutionize the domestic sphere.

> **" THE HOUSE IS A MACHINE FOR living IN."**

Corbusier included the Maison Dom-Ino of 1915 in his manifesto but his first new house-type was what he called the Immeuble-villa, intended as the main form of housing in his first city plan. Clearly derived from the monks' cells at Ema, the Immeuble-villa was a maisonette unit with a double height living space, alongside which was placed a garden. Corbusier's intention was for each unit to be stacked vertically or horizontally to create small housing blocks.

The Immeuble-villa was exhibited as a prototype for mass-produced housing at the 1925 Exposition des Arts Decoratifs in Paris. Entitled the *Pavillon de l' Esprit Nouveau* it offered a clear statement of the visual language of the new architecture. Rectangular in form, it is flat-roofed, its plain white concrete surface left unadorned by ornament. Large expanses of window brought light into the open-plan spaces of the interior. In keeping with Purist principles, it was furnished with what Corbusier called objet-types, like the bentwood chairs, objects which were not consciously styled but whose form had through use evolved into the perfect design. On the walls were hung Purist paintings.

As a concept the Pavillon perfectly combined the engineer's aesthetic with artistic sensibility. Its display at a major French exhibition also assured Corbusier of the publicity which he assiduously cultivated throughout his life.

Vers une Architecture contained designs for a second prototype dwelling, the Maison Citrohan. Again Corbusier played on words to convey the element of mass production and standardization in his work. Here was a house designed to work as efficiently and economically as a car. In many respects it was very similar to the Immeuble-villa. A white box, it contains a double height living space with mezzanine floor for the parents' rooms. Further bedrooms and a solarium are placed on the top floor. The main space of the house was lit by vast windows made from factory produced glazing. The most dramatic innovation in the Citrohan house was its elevation from the ground, supported on stilts or "pilotis". Again, this house-type would be built as a prototype for an exhibition. At the Weissenhof Siedlung, the display of model houses designed by leading European modernists which was held in Stuttgart in 1927, Corbusier contributed one single and one pair of houses built on the Citrohan method.

Corbusier hoped that these house-types would form the basis of a mass housing programme to meet the severe housing shortage in Europe at this date. But despite his hard work and the promotion of his ideas at exhibitions and in print he only built one scheme of workers' housing in the inter-war period, at Pessac, near Bordeaux (1924–26). The vast majority of his work in the 1920s was the design of villas (which he worked on with his partner in practice, his cousin Pierre Jeanneret) for a very different clientele: wealthy, *haute-bourgeoise* families and individuals, many of whom were part of the Paris art world. People, in fact, very like Corbusier himself.

The villas he built during the 1920s all relied for their basic structure and spatial form on elements of the Maison Dom-Ino and the Maison Citrohan, but for their appearance Corb developed a basic grammar of expression which he published in 1926, the "Five Points of a New Architecture":

1 **PILOTIS:** to lift the house off the ground.

2 **THE FREE PLAN:** the framed construction of the building allowing the interior space to be organized as desired.

3 **THE FREE FACADE:** since the external walls were not load-bearing, they could be divided up wherever necessary by windows and other apertures.

4 **THE RIBBON WINDOW:** a long horizontal window.

5 **THE ROOF GARDEN:** intended to replace the ground covered by the house and bring its inhabitants into a direct relationship with nature.

The Villa Stein de Monzie at Garches near Paris of 1926 exemplifies the 5 Points. The clients wanted a modern home to match their collection of modern art, and that is certainly what they got. On the front elevation can be seen the ribbon windows, free facade and roof terrace dictated by the 5 Points. The rear facade incorporates the staircase of the Maison Citrohan, which allows a complicated interplay of advancing and receding forms.

To enter the house one passes under a canopy which, in a clear statement of the machine aesthetic, recalls the struts and wings of an aeroplane. From here one steps into a 4-columned hall which is suffused with light from the ribbon windows and the stairwell above. A spiral staircase leads up to the main floor of the house, a large open living room with a terrace, the exemplar of Corbusier's desire to make man, machine and nature co-exist.

The Villa Savoye, in Poissy, of 1929–31 represents the highpoint of purist architecture and is a sophisticated blend of Corbusier's machine aesthetic and his interest in a more abstract, classical and poetic use of form.

When first built, the house stood in the middle of a field like a classical villa set in an ideal landscape. On this expanse of verdure the house seems to hover, an impression enhanced by each designed to serve a particular function. For relaxation there was the chaise longue; for conversation, the *"chaise à dossier basculante"* and for enjoying a glass of port after dinner, the modernized version of the club armchair, the *"grand confort"*. Though their functions were differentiated they shared the same Purist vocabulary of metal frame and leather or canvas upholstery. They complemented perfectly the spare, open spaces of villas like the Villa Savoye.

Corbusier's interest in what went inside the house, as well as the house itself, reminds us of the breadth of his vision. The reform of the house and its contents was just one component of his desire to replan the city as a whole.

THE CITY OF TOMORROW

Corbusier began working on ideas for reforming the design of towns in 1915, inspired, perhaps, by Garnier's example. By 1922 he had produced the first of his schemes for a modern city, the *Ville Contemporaine*, a plan which laid down the main principles which would inform all his subsequent schemes.

The starting point for Corbusier's city designs was a critique of the existing nineteenth-century city – a chaotic, unorganized mess, riddled with slums and from which nature had been eliminated. In its place, he proposed a zoned city in which individual elements such as housing, industry, administration occupied a specific area; the whole connected by networks of transportation for cars, trains and air travel. To bring nature back into the city, the modern technologies of reinforced concrete would allow the building of tall blocks of housing and offices. The land released by building high could then be used for parks.

The plans for the *Ville Contemporaine*, a city for 3 million inhabitants, has all these features. At the heart of the plan is a traffic terminal surrounded by a central commercial district of 24 glass skyscrapers. This is then followed by housing for the managers and bureaucrats who would work in these glass towers. A green belt of land separates this area of the city from the manufacturing area and a further belt divides this from the housing for those who worked in the city's factories.

Constructed from concrete and steel the plan was an attempt to demonstrate how technology could allow high-density living yet at the same time bring light, space and greenery to all through the provision of high-rise housing. However health-giving the plan may have been it was also extremely elitist. The managers and their ilk were to live in the centre, the ordinary worker was relegated to the suburb. At this date, Corbusier was more interested in meritocracy than democracy or socialism, however much he may later have pretended otherwise.

Corbusier put his first ideas on town planning into print in 1925 as *Urbanisme* (translated as *"The City of Tomorrow"*). In the same year he exhibited alongside the *Pavillon de l' Esprit Nouveau* a scheme for the replanning of a part of Paris to the north of the Ile de la Cité. In his *Plan Voisin pour Paris* (the *Voisin* derives from Corbusier's sponsor for the project, an aeroplane manufacturer), he proposed the complete demolition of the site and the construction of a miniature version of the *Ville Contemporaine*, complete with glass skyscrapers. Such a ruthless disregard for an historic area of Paris, not surprisingly, meant the scheme remained unbuilt.

Corbusier continued to work on urban planning throughout the 1920s. By the beginning of the 1930s it had become one of his chief interests. This phase saw another grand city plan, the *Ville Radieuse* (1935), like the *Ville Contemporaine*, a theoretical model intended for universal application.

The *Ville Radieuse*, or Radiant City, borrowed many of its elements from the *Ville Contemporaine*. The buildings were raised on pilotis and the office blocks were again skyscrapers. But in important aspects it was very different. The *Ville Contemporaine* had been organized as a series of concentric rings but the Radiant City was a linear city, each function was set into a separate parallel band. Different too was the arrangement of housing, with one single classless district at the centre of the plan, separated from the business zone and the industrial zone by strips of parkland. The housing was also less luxurious than the Immeuble-villa of 1922. Corbusier's politics had become less elitist since the early 1920s!

Despite being a much more practical and economical plan than any of his previous attempts Corbusier's hopes that it might be realized were not to be met. In a period of economic depression it was unlikely that such a scheme could be enacted and in any case, it required a vast greenfield site. No such location would become available until after World War Two which was, of course, when many of his urban ideas would be explored and put into practice.

TOWARDS A MONUMENTAL ARCHITECTURE

By the 1930s Corbusier had become a well-known figure, a status which led to a number of important commissions. In this work may be seen the beginnings of a reworking of the aesthetic principles of Purism, a process which would culminate in the more emotional and powerful architecture of the post-war years and a return to the vernacular which had characterized his earliest works.

The Pavillon Suisse, of 1930–31, a residential block to house international students visiting Paris, was a key building in the transition to a new phase of design. In its use of form and materials it represents a reworking of the 5 Points and the conventions Corbusier had used in his villa designs of the 1920s. In place of the still and pure geometric forms of the Villas Savoye or Stein, a grander and more powerful architectural language can be seen in the contrast between the rectangular box which houses the students' rooms and the smaller block, with a curved frontage, which abuts onto the main building and contains a staircase tower and student lounge.

Corbusier's approach to materials also changed. Though the main block is carried on pilotis, these are very different from those at the Villa Savoye. Not sleek and circular in section but irregular in form; their concrete structure left bare and unpainted. Perhaps the most dramatic element of the design is the rubble wall of the student lounge, the first thing seen when approaching the Pavillon.

This aggrandizement of the 5 Points and the use of untreated concrete surfaces may be partly explained by the fact that the Pavillon was a public building, something for which a more monumental architectural language than that of Purism was appropriate. But it also had much to do with Corbusier's constant search for new and evolving forms of modern architecture; a process which would reach its finest expression after the end of war in 1945.

BRUTALISM AND SPIRITUALITY: THE POST-WAR WORK

The first commission he received once war was over must have felt like an act of vindication to Corbusier. After years of developing prototypes for mass housing which were never realized, the French government asked him to design a new prototype for mass dwelling as part of their plans to meet the post-war housing shortage which, as in most parts of Europe, was acute. This became the *Unité d' Habitation*, the culmination of all Corbusier's pre-war ideas about housing and the city combined into one building.

The Unité is a massive block and stands on a raised site overlooking the city of Marseille. A cheap dwelling both to build and to live in, Corbusier wrote that the block would: "provide with silence and solitude before the sun, space and greenery, a dwelling which will be the perfect receptacle for the family".

Its design is simple. It is like a gigantic concrete bottle rack into which are slotted units for living and leisure, shopping and education. It contains a variety of apartment types, most with a double height living room which looks onto a balcony, all accessed from corridors or "streets" which run through the centre of the block. Dotted around the block are the various amenities which transform it from being a mere dwelling place into a living community. Halfway up are hotels and shops. There are also clubs and meeting rooms, whilst on the roof are recreation facilities.

The appearance of the Unité represents the further monumentalization of the 5 Points which he had initiated at the Pavillon Suisse. This time the block is carried on huge pilotis that look like elephants' legs and, as in the rest of the block, the concrete from which they were made is left untreated. This is known as *beton brut*; and is the main technique in which Corbusier would build from this date. It gives the name to this period of his work, Brutalism.

The overall effect of the Unité is of a massive piece of sculpture; a monument to and celebration of the ordinary people who would live in the block. It was a very successful building and immediately caught the imagination of young architects across Europe. Re-worked versions of the scheme can be found in countless post-war housing estates, the Alton West estate in west London of 1955–60 being a particularly notable example.

Corbusier explored this Brutalist aesthetic throughout the 1950s. He succeeded in forging from such a raw and visceral material as concrete the most beautiful and spiritual buildings. The church of Notre-Dame du Haut at Ronchamp exemplifies this practice. It was built to replace a pilgrimage chapel destroyed during the war. The new church sits on the brow of a hill, a magnificent organic structure. It has a reinforced concrete frame topped by a concrete roof, which looks just like the underside of a mushroom. In a touching act of remembrance the walls incorporate brick and rubble from the destroyed church. The interior is outstanding. Corbusier's concern was to create a sacred and very special space. This he achieved by the creation of a cavernous area and a careful filtering of natural light though specially designed windows. From the exterior the windows appear as tiny slits in the wall which are filled with stained glass. Inside they open out into large bays funnelling the jewel-coloured light into the chapel.

This sense of spirituality was continued at another commission for a religious group, the Dominican Monastery of Saint Marie de la Tourette, near Lyons. Onto the slope of a hill Corbusier placed an elevated square building which incorporated the monks' cells, a chapel and refectory. The upper section consists of two rows of monks' cells, clearly articulated on the exterior, beneath are the communal rooms – the classrooms and the refectories – this tier encircled by corridors with walls which resemble Japanese screens. The whole structure focuses inwards onto a cloister. Again much use of light is made through the use of screens and slit like windows to give a spiritual quality to the building. At the same time the concrete architecture creates an appropriately ascetic environment for the monks.

This new aesthetic was to receive its greatest challenge when Corbusier was invited, along with the British architects Jane Drew and Maxwell Fry, to design a new city for the Punjab region of India, to be named Chandigarh. Corbusier designed the city plan of Chandigarh as well as four government buildings and several monuments. The outstanding building is the High Court with its dramatically projecting roof and grid-like facade; a "decorative" feature created by the deep-projecting balconies, or *brise-soleils*, which shelter the inhabitants from the heat of the sun.

The brutalist aesthetic also found expression in private commissions, most notably the Maisons Jaoul at Neuilly-sur-Seine (1951–55). There are two houses, set at right angles to each other, each consisting of a concrete tunnel vaulted living space, the vaults carried on brick walls, all the surfaces being left rough. In their mixing of brick and wood these houses represent a return to the love of nature which we saw in Corbusier's earliest works.

Corbusier died in 1965. Since then his reputation has suffered at the hands of those who would hold him solely responsible for the problems of our post-war cities; though he had no control over the way his ideas would be used. But if we look again at his ideas, his designs, at what he was trying to achieve in his work, the beauty of his architecture and its challenging nature is still as fresh and full of impact as it was when it was first built.

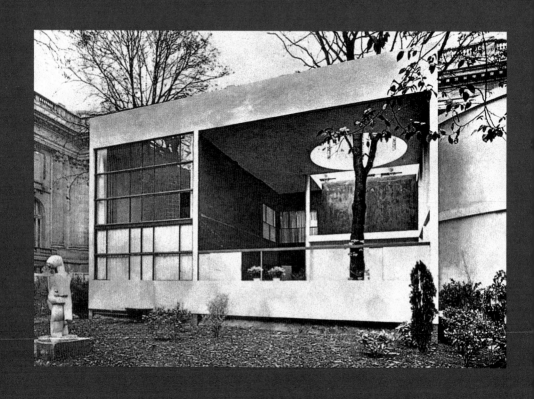

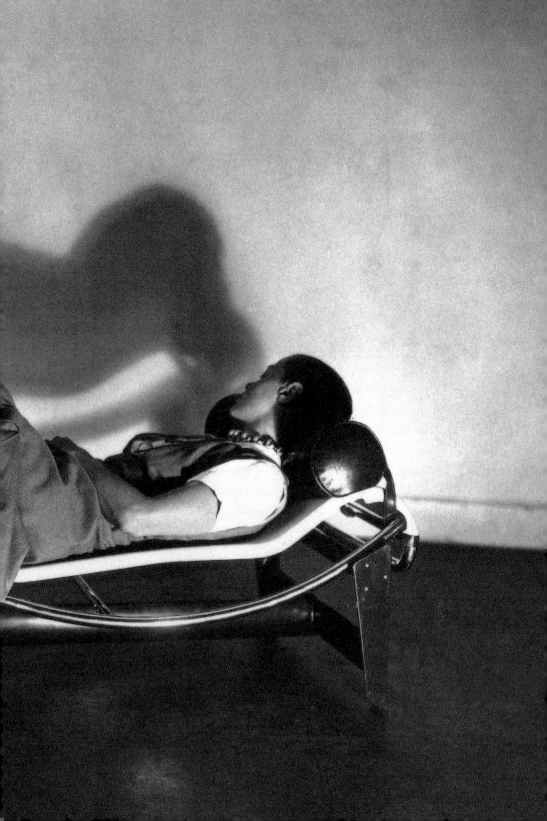

UNIVERSITÉ DE PARIS · FONDATION SUISSE

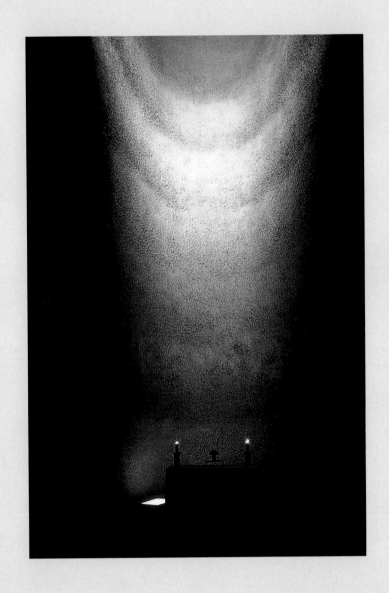

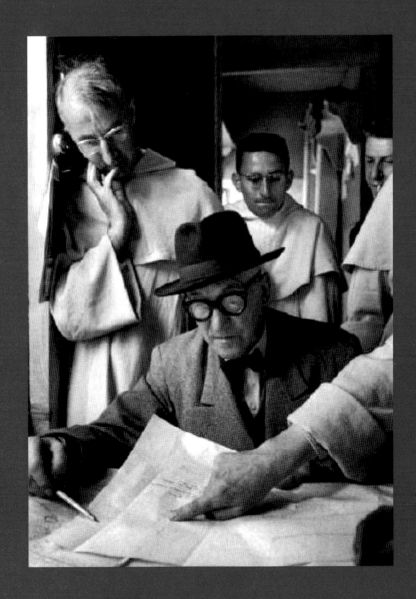

CITE DE REFUGE

The entrance to the Cité de Refuge (Salvation Army hostel) in Paris. This was one of the first of Corbusier's works in which he sought to transform the language of Purism into a more monumental idiom.

COMMUNION WITH NATURE

The open roof terrace of the Villa Savoye with the ramp leading to the solarium. Through techniques such as these Corbusier hoped to reintegrate people and nature.

THE PAINTER

Corbusier seated before one of his paintings. Throughout his life he used the medium of art to help him in his search for a new visual language for architecture.

CONCRETE

The archetypal modern material for Corbusier was concrete. In his later Brutalist works like this, the Chapel at Ronchamp, Corbusier exploited the sculptural possiblilities of this material to visceral effect.

MUSEUM IN ZURICH

In the country of his birth, Corbusier designed this small pavilion to house a collection of his work.

CORBUSIER'S APARTMENT/VILLA FALLET

Left: a typical Corbusian motif: a spiral staircase used as the route through and into the double height space of an interior. Right: Corbusier's first commission in his home town of Chaux.

VILLA SCHWOB

The classicism in plan and style of this villa reflects the influence of Corbusier's Voyage d'Orient.

MAISON OZENFANT/MAISONS JAOUL

Left and top right: the studio and house Corbusier designed for his collaborator in Purism, Amédée Ozenfant. Its abstract forms contrast with (bottom right) the vernacular inspired interior of the Maison Jaoul, designed in the Brutalist phase of his career.

MAISON LAROCHE/JEANNERET

Interior (left) and main facade (right) of a pair of houses for two typical Corbusier clients: his brother, Albert and a collector of modern art, Raoul La Roche. Such patrons allowed him the freedom to produce daring designs like these.

PAVILLON DE L'ESPRIT NOUVEAU/MAISON COOK

Two dwellings that embody Corbusier's love of types and rules. The Pavillion (left) was a built prototype of the immeuble-villa, the mass-produceable housing unit for the Ville Contemporaine. The Maison Cook (right) demonstrates Corbusier's "Five Points".

VILLA STEIN/DE MONZIE

A modern house to match the clients' collection of modern art. Corbusier's machine aesthetic is evident her in the canopy over the door which recalls the struts of an aeroplane wing.

THE EMBODIMENT OF PURISM

The Villa Savoye was the most perfect expression of Purism's combination of abstraction and the principles of classicism.

THE MODERN INTERIOR

As in a classical villa, the entrace hall (bottom left) of the Villa Savoye acts as the prelude to the *piano nobile* (main floor) of the house. This contains the salon (top left), a large living space overlooking the roof terrace, and the bathroom (right), reflecting the importance Corbusier attached to hygiene.

THE CHAIR IS A MACHINE FOR SITTING IN

Just as Corbusier zoned the functions of the city so he distinguished among the different purposes funiture served. The Grand Confort (left) was for the gentlemen relaxing after dinner while the fauteuil à dossier basculant allowed its occupant to lean back and enjoy converstaion

CHAISE LONGUE

Another chair type, this time for reclining upon. Here Corbusier's co-designer of furniture, Charlotte Perriand, demonstrates one of the positions into which the Chaise could be set.

MODEL HOUSES

At the Weissenhof Siedlung, a model estate of modernist houses erected in Stuttgart in 1927, Corbusier contributed these houses: built versions of the house-type, the Maison Citrohan.

REWORKING PURISM

At the Pavillon Suisse, Corbusier began to turn away from the simplicity and immateriality of Purism towards a more monumental treatment of form. This is evident in the entrance block of the Pavillon (left) with the introduction of new materials like stone to Corbusier's repertoire, and the chunky treatment of the pilotis (top right.)

UNITÉ D'HABITATION

The culmination of all Corbusier's ideas about the house and the city, combined into one building. The Unité was a prototype housing block that combined maisonettes, internal streets, shops and other facilities to create a community in the sky.

TRANSFORMING THE FIVE POINTS

Although the Unité is designed in the language of Brutalism, the Five Points remained a guiding principle underpinning the design. The block has a roof terrace that incorporates a swimming pool.

A RICHER LANGUAGE

The entrance lobby of the Unité (top left) and the details of the facades are characteristic of Corbusier's post-war Brutalism.

UNITÉ INTERIORS

The maisonettes at the Unité recall the monks' cells at Ema which Corbusier saw as a young man on his journey of self-education.

NOTRE DAME DU HAUT, RONCHAMP

Built on the site of a pilgrimage chapel destroyed during the war, Corbusier's new building is a manificent and awe-inspiring organic structure.

RONCHAMP IN DETAIL

These details show the sculptural possibilities Corbusier derived from his use of concrete.

BRUTALISM AND SPIRITUALITY

Inside the massive walls of Notre Dame du Haut lies the cavernous space of the chapel. Its haunting atmosphere is enhanced by the funnel windows which filter light into the interior.

THE MONASTERY OF SAINT MARIE DE LA TOURETTE

A second religious commission for Corbusier. The Monastery's design picks up on many of the themes explored at Ronchamp although here the theme is the rectilinear rather than the organic.

BELFRY AT TOURETTE/CORBUSIER

The wall upon the belfry perches (left) shows the untreated use of concrete that characterizes Brutalism. Right: Corbusier explains his work to the monks of the monastery.

CHAPEL AT TOURETTE

As at Ronchamp Corbusier makes wonderful use of directional light and dramatic wall surfaces to create a sense of spirituality.

CORBUSIER IN INDIA

In 1950 Corbusier was invited to become the master planner of the new state capital of the Punjab, Chandigarh. The Palace of Assembly (left) was one of the two public buildings he designed there. The sweeping forms of its roof help shade the interior (right) from the intense heat outside.

PALACE OF ASSEMBLY, CHANDIGARH/ MAISONS JAOUL, PARIS

Left: the sculptural forms of the Palace of Assembly's roof. Right: in this pair of houses outside Paris Corbusier returned to the vernacular traditions of his very first work.

CARPENTER CENTER/VILLA SHODAN

Left: the Carpenter Centre for the Visual Arts at Harvard University was one of Corbusier's last works and his only North American commission. Right: Villa Shodan, Ahmedabad. While in India, Corbusier also worked in the city of Ahmedabad, an important centre of India's textile trade.

Picture credits

The publishers would like to thank the following sources for
their kind permission to reproduce the pictures in this book:

AKG, London/ Paul Almasy 51, 73, Erich Lessing 45, Schutze/Rodemann 58
Architectural Association Photo Library/S. Buerger 75, L. Gasson 1, Martin Jones 38b,
    P. Keirle 26, S. Prasad 34, 35t, R.Whitehouse 33, F.R. Yerbury 31, 32
Arcaid 7/Richard Bryant 2, Dennis Gilbert 30, Paul Raftery 28, 29t, 36, 38t, 39,
    50, 52, 55, 56, 57
"Cassina I Maestri" Collection, Cassina S.p.A./photo: Oliviero Venturi 40, photo Andrea
    Zani 41
Edifice/Darley 44, 46, 48, Lewis 74, Schneebelie 60
Robert Harding Picture Library Ltd. 29b/C. Gascoigne 70, 72, K.Hart 62, P. Koch 8
Lucien Hervé 5, 24, 25, 35b, 47b
Hulton Getty 54 t,b/Ernst Haas 71
The Image Bank/Archive Photos 64, 66, 68
Magnum Photos/Rene Burri 4, 67, Marc Riboud 61
©Charlotte Perriand 42
Roger-Viollet 47t

Every effort has been made to acknowledge correctly and contact the source and/copyright
holder of each picture, and Carlton Books Limited apologises for any unintentional errors
or omissions which will be corrected in future editions of this book.